Blackbirds

GREG SANTOS

BLACK-BIRDS

 **Goggles**
EYEWEAR PAMPHLET SERIES 2018

First published in 2018
by Eyewear Publishing Ltd
Suite 333, 19-21 Crawford Street
Marylebone, London W1H 1PJ
United Kingdom

Typeset with graphic design by Edwin Smet
Author photo by Studio Duda
Printed in England by Lightning Source

ISBN 978-1-912477-44-9

*The editor has generally followed Canadian spelling
and punctuation at the author's request.*

WWW.EYEWEARPUBLISHING.COM

para mi familia

TABLE OF CONTENTS

👓 Goggles

I – BLACKBIRDS

I have become a brother of jackals,
a companion of owls.
My skin grows black and peels;
my body burns with fever.
My lyre is tuned to mourning,
and my pipe to the sound of wailing.

– Job 30:29-31

AT THE ROOM OF EXTINCT SPECIES ON MY DAUGHTER'S SIX-MONTH BIRTHDAY

Musée National d'Histoire Naturelle, Paris

Over there, a colossal egg
from the elephant bird of Madagascar.

Holding my daughter close, I notice
her head is half the size of the egg.

I feel an overwhelming ache
that goes back millions of years.

My daughter babbles in the darkness.
I want to coddle the egg, hug its insides.

I HAVE A PROBLEM

All I care about is everything.
I like to lie down and look up at the stars,
even when there are none.
I am almost nothing but thoughts and water.
I find mirrors unbearably off-putting.
My children find them droll.
Do you feel that too?
My left hand feels like a cataclysmic storm.
I will never tire of looking at my wife.
Her smile is like a constant sonar beep
in the depths of my chest.
I hear rain even when it's sunny out.
Have you ever squinted at the ocean
so the sky and the water blend until
you don't know where one ends and the other begins?
I'm doing that right now with you.

SIEM REAP, CAMBODIA

Before stepping into a taxi
a young girl struggles to take the city with her:

Warm, sticky air bathing the street market,
comforting scent of fragrant rice,
pungent odor of dry fish,
raw flesh hung on butchers' hooks,
squawking of chickens in rusty wire prisons,
crescendo of rickshaws, scooters, bicycles;
the city she will no longer call home.

As she speeds away, the city recedes into memory,
as does the rolling countryside,
once dotted by women tending to the paddies,
children splashing among water buffalo.

Now, echoes of distant missiles pierce her memories,
murders of crows dive into reddened fields.

The faces of Angkor watch sadly
as their city crumbles,
as another one of their children flees,
taking nothing with her but me,
gently growing inside.

ABUELOS

60 years of marriage
and they still flirt with each other.

After reading ¡Hola!
where they can learn all the latest news

on the Spanish royals, then tuning into
Wheel of Fortune, *The Price is Right*,

she, with her hearing aid turned off
(the batteries died long ago),

he, constantly glancing out the window
to see if anyone's blocked the garage.

They have coffee together every day,
heating the Nescafé and milk

in the microwave, a metal tin of cookies
always within reaching distance.

When she cooks, it is her domain.
'Luciano, get the potatoes!'

He'll shuffle downstairs, lug the potatoes
up the stairs, down the stairs.

'Luciano, cut the prosciutto!' Back upstairs,
to the metal slicing machine, a Christmas gift.

They attempt to keep the squirrels away
with glass shards in their vegetable garden,

yet they always come back. A neighbour
suggested they use Zugar brand fertilizer.

My grandfather snapped back that sugar does nothing
to help the garden but give the squirrels tooth decay.

SOUND MACHINE

I lie on our bed,
a buoy atop tranquil waters.

You are downstairs
preparing the baby's food.

Hum of the microwave,
a distant motorboat.

I flow in and out of sleep,
waking to sounds of the kitchen:

clink of a spoon
navigating glass,

syncopations of drawers
opening and closing.

Our child is asleep
like driftwood.

Pillows propped around her,
preventing her tiny frame

from drifting out to sea
on a wayward tide.

ADOPTION

after Rita Joe

I lost my talk when you asked me how I liked this country.

When you remarked that I was the only Asian student in class,
even when I explained I was from here but adopted.

When you pulled your eyes into slits.
When you slapped your chest, *beep beep*, called me Sulu.

When you said it was a shame that I wasn't teaching my daughter my
         native language,
after I told you we spoke English at home.

When I came into the store to buy cookies
and you told me to get out because no one had ordered any Chinese food.

When I was in kindergarten and you told my mother
that she wasn't my real mother because I didn't look like her.

I found my talk when my mother asked you to touch her arm,
and when you did, she said, *Now do I feel real to you?*

INSOMNIACS

The neon moon
burns a circle
into the carpet.

My infant daughter
slumps gently in my arms.

Neither of us can sleep.

I feel her heart
flutter like tiny
blackbirds
against my chest.

It is otherwise quiet.

The universe
has been good to me.

LITANY

Dad was born in Cascais.
Mom was born in Madrid.

My grandfather, born in Trieste,
which until that year was part of Austria.

I was born in Montreal,
to anonymous Cambodian refugees.

My grandfather's last name is Cervi.
When Trieste was annexed to Italy,

the Cervis were forced to change their name.
My grandfather forgets what his name used to be.

My family is from forgetfulness,
our geography forever shifting.

AIR RAID

Paris, France

I wake up to the sounds
of air raid sirens and sparrows.

Our child sleeps through it all.
I am both relieved and jealous.

The clothes are wrung,
hanging out to dry like animal skins.

Eager, I devour my cold cuts.
I have slept in again.

Tomorrow will be different,
I lie to myself.

The dishwasher is convulsing
with laughter.

LISBOA

I saw Vasco da Gama's
tomb today.

Bought Luis de Camões'
collected lyric poems.

Saw Camões' tomb,
drank Coke from a glass bottle.

Then had my wallet stolen on the tram.
Didn't feel any lighter.

Got completely lost
on the streets of Portugal.

Recovered some dignity:
found a bus to Belém.

Ate the world's best
custard tarts.

Still, scribbling away
next to my sleeping wife and daughter.

I didn't discover a passage to India
but all things considered,

a good day
is a good day.

BERRY PICKING

In August
red caps would ripen
in the forest
behind my house.

Bringing wicker baskets
lined with white napkins –
left open like
treasure maps.

We were explorers
snapping stalks,
crunching branches
beneath our feet.

Many of the fruits were
already eaten by animals,
their buds left
bleaching in the sun.

On a good day
we'd kneel in the dirt,
part the leaves and dig up
clusters of red jewels.

We'd fold napkins
over the delicate berries,
the paper stained
with fresh blood.

AT THE COTTAGE

'Daddy, is that a shooting star line?'

'No,' I say. 'It's from a plane.
But it does look like a comet tail.'

My son wants a closer look at the stars
before heading to bed.

I step outside barefoot, his three-year-old body
nestled into my chest.

In the city it's rare to glimpse
more than the moon at night.

We both look up,
wordless for a minute or so,
our necks craned, two odd bird silhouettes.

'The stars,' he's searching for the right words,
'the stars, some of them are planets?'

He mulls the idea over,
a marble of possibilities,
rolling it around in his head.

'The earth is not up there.
The earth is... the earth is... on the ground.'
I nod, hugging him tighter.

Satisfied, my son waves and says,
'Goodnight stars.'

We watch the white jet trail
streaking across the sky.

II – SOMETHING CLICKED

A profound silence reigned also in the sky:
the birds had ceased their songs.

Omega: The Last Days of the World,
Camille Flammarion

Goggles

ERASURE

The sky is a deflated balloon.
The children are spinning, compass needles on the fritz.

The world's beaches, shucked out to sea.
The grass-seed devouring sparrows have flown off.

There's a hole where the sun used to be.
No use cleaning off the graffiti in the alleyway.

What's the use of cleaning anything anymore?
One last poutine for the road.

Live-tweeting the apocalypse is one helluva pastime, you say.
More like a vocation, my voice an echo.

HANGRY

This raspberry/peach yogurt tastes bitter.
Why does everything taste bitter today?

The headlines say science can explain why people are jerks.
Here are 20 great ways to sabotage yourself.

I misread 'so many people killing it this month'
as 'so many people killing this month'.

I swore while making burnt grilled-cheese sandwiches for lunch.
I don't know what to make of the news anymore.

How do we respond to this horrible day?
I watched a video of how instant ramen noodles are made.

👓 Goggles

MURICA

Rumor has it we are going to raise a barn.
Stay tuned. Have a beverage with me.

Pepsi says LIVE FOR NOW.
Living for corn syrup is vexing.

Our little American town is exhausted.
Please help.

CONSIDERING HANSEL AND GRETEL

Do you see the moon?
It follows you wherever you are.

Come back inside.
The teeth are chattering.

Splatters on an apron.
Stay home, dears.

The TV is bursting with bones,
lost children & BBQs.

I dream of a one-way
trip to Mars.

I leave a trail of crumbs
for monsters are not impossible.

Goggles

THE OTHER SIDE

Deaths in the evening, births in the morning.
Homely are the tuxedos for family mourning.

I'll always remember when you touched my heart:
it was gelatinous and smelled vaguely of René Descartes.

I'm glad I disassembled you and put you back together.
I bought the turkey dinner made from imitation leather.

Where's a rotten egg when you need one?
I know of a metaphysical preacher named Donne.

It is not a cactus or a cheese curd or a shroud.
Look through the telescope: it's the Large Magellanic Cloud!

Let us raise our flamethrowers in celebration!
I have joined the national aeronautics and space administration.

CRACKING UP

Waiting by a crosswalk, we watched a motorcyclist zoom by.
The ground shook like an elephant caught in a draft,
prompting me to contemplate the fragility of the cosmos.

We were holding hands, happy to feel the breeze on our faces.
Being somewhat of a wind connoisseur, I noticed a hint of ginger
with a delicate bouquet of foreboding. But I kept it to myself.

A bony woman with a droopy face came up to us and asked,
'Excuse me, were you two laughing at me?'
M and I looked at each other, a bit shocked by the question.

'No,' I said. The droopy-faced woman blinked and nodded.
'Oh,' she said, 'sorry about that. I have low self-esteem. Have a nice day.'
And then she droopily shuffled off.

'I didn't think we were laughing at her, were we?' I asked.
'Oh no,' M said, 'I wasn't laughing at all.'
At a traffic light, we stared absentmindedly at the colored circles.

They looked like brightly lit cough drops. 'You know,' I said guiltily,
'I might have been giggling a little under my breath.'
'Yeah,' M said, 'me too.'

A pick-up truck nearby ran the red light and almost hit a man
crossing on the other side of the street.
M and I couldn't hold it back any longer and we burst out laughing.

Our sides hurt so much, everything began shaking uncontrollably.
Soon dandelions in sidewalk cracks were bent over in hysterics,
skyscrapers were leaning on each others' shoulders and howling,

planets could be heard slapping their knees, even the Milky Way was spewing dairy out its nose... And this is the way the world ends. Not with a bang. Certainly not with a whimper. But with a chortle.

GENTLEMAN STROLLER OF CITY STREETS

Sunglasses, dress shirt, pants.
Strolling all grey by The Ritz.
Don Draper of the sidewalk.
The stop hand winks at me red.

The buzz of a double-decker bus.
Montreal is not New York or London
but it might as well be.
Hey, it's Fernando Pessoa's birthday!

It's dawned on me.
A real man should be manifest in time.
The art of man isn't hard to master
but playing the part is a disaster.

Elevator rides, networking, meetings.
Wait. Wait for the walking man.
The allure to be 'The Man'
is seductive, deadly.

That Draper fellow
has it all figured out.
There's a good reason
he sports designer shades.

I have a terrible poker face.
This pair was a carnival giveaway.
I'm bound to get caught.
Please, have a rum and Coke with me.

Swizzle sticks, pizzazz, bravura.
Looking the part is only part of the key.
But an old-fashioned does not a man make.
A man shouldn't mean but be.

CLICKBAIT

Despite the headlines,
life is good.

How might the human face appear in 100,000 years?
Have you ever considered how many brains there are in the world?

I like how the Internet is starting to look.
Climb larger and larger mental states.

You are a child in a house that is warm.
So very much in love.

A, C, G, T danced on typewriter ribbon
and something clicked.

Goggles

III – LOST & FOUND

When it is dark enough, you can see the stars.

Attributed to Charles A. Beard

IN TIMES OF TRAGEDY

a blackout poem

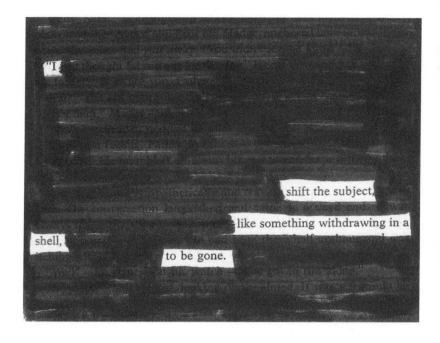

"I

shift the subject,

like something withdrawing in a

shell,

to be gone.

Goggles

I'M DOG. WHO ARE YOU?

People who thought differently were called worms, dogs, traitors.

– from an article in The New York Times on the fallout of the Khmer Rouge and the Cambodian genocide

I.
Once in a hospital waiting room with my father,
another child kept turning around to look at me,
singing *ching chong chow!*

His tinny song went on and on.
I did not know how to react.
Ignoring the boy did nothing.

My first response was to bare my teeth,
bark, bark, bark! I grinned, wild-eyed.
The boy hid. My father stared.

II.
When my children were younger they used to scream,
terrorized, running in the opposite
direction when any canine strolled by.

In Cambodia, they once feared
Vach du Mach, One with the Gun,
coward who killed millions, his own people.

Words were used as knives.
Children would turn in their parents.
The wrong sentence was a life sentence.

III.
Cuddling my whiskered face up to theirs,
today my kids knead my fur in their tiny hands.
They call it puppy love.

Who are you?
I'm dog. I embrace my dogness.
Are you dog, too?

Goggles

NOUS SOMMES PARIS

Alert
At home
We hid under a desk

Outraged
Firebombed
Brutally threatened

Somber
Darkest day
Disappearing

*

Bolstered
Pledge
Let us unite

Tell the media
Defend art
We will win

Waving pens and papers
Armed and dangerous
Final *coup de grâce*

MIGRATION

The harbor, black with people surging in from the streets. The sea, frothing and slamming against the stone retaining walls. Countless figures losing their footing from algae and seaweed.

The skyline, teeming with airships, searchlights scanning the cityscape. The last remaining boat swells from the weight of its passengers. Families, shouting and jostling to get on board. Scores of bodies dropping into the water, ants falling into an inkwell.

A disembodied voice calls for the anchor to be hoisted. On shore the scraping of rusty chains, barely heard over the crowd.

Shoulder to shoulder, features blending with the others on the boat. All silent, they look toward those left on the pier.

The crowd, condemned beast with thousands of eyes, each following the lone ship as it rounds the cape and vanishes.

Goggles

NOVEMBER 10, 2016

a villanelle

I can't stop myself from crying.
It's time for the curtain call.
Cohen is dead, Trump is president.

It's hard to step out of Mount Royal's
shadow when I'm only an ant.
I can't stop myself from crying.

Tried to walk out from under him.
He taught me how to don my hat.
Cohen is dead, Trump is president.

My aunt gave me *Flowers for Hitler*
before I knew poetry's song.
I can't stop myself from crying.

I now give him this slight bouquet.
His was the template I tried to break.
Cohen is dead, Trump is president.

2016, I'm done with you.
All you are is emotional ruin.
I can't stop myself from crying.
Cohen is dead, Trump is president.

OUR BLOOD SPANS CONTINENTS

We streaming rivers,
the Saint Lawrence,
the Tagus,
the Mississippi
the Tigris,
the Mekong.

> We émigrés,
> we exiles,
> we fugitives,
> we displaced persons,
> we asylum seekers
> we boat people.

> > Whatever you call us,
> > we span oceans.

You collect donations,
you collect blankets,
you collect winter hats,
you collect hoodies,
you collect tube socks,
you collect toothpaste,
you collect long-distance phone cards.

> You round up what you take for granted,
> what we need to survive to feel human again.

We cannot be claimed or owned.
We cannot be cast away or sent back.

Goggles

We long for a home that can never be home again.

We reluctant
nomads.

We are submarine, adrift amid the tides.
Our roots are not held down by dirt or stones.

Shrugging off nations' clothes,
naked, flowing, we are molten.

'At the Room of Extinct Species on my Daughter's Six-Month Birthday' appeared in *Encore Literary Magazine*.

'I Have a Problem' appeared in *The Walrus*.

'Litany' and 'Migration' appeared in *Ricepaper Magazine*.

'Siem Reap, Cambodia' and 'Adoption' appeared in *Cha: An Asian Literary Journal*.

'Abuelos' appeared in *Queen's Quarterly*.

'Insomniacs' appeared in *The New Haven Review*.

'Air Raid' and 'Lisboa' appeared in *Scrivener Creative Review*.

'Berry Picking' appeared as a limited edition broadside through ImPress in 2006.

'Erasure' appeared in *Enclave*.

'Hangry' and 'Considering Hansel and Gretel' appeared in *Cosmonauts Avenue*.

'Murica' appeared in *Metatron*.

'The Other Side' appeared in *The Week Shall Inherit the Verse*.

'Cracking Up' appeared in *New Wave Vomit*.

'Gentleman Stroller of City Streets' and 'November 10, 2016' appeared in *Matrix*.

'Clickbait' appeared in *This Zine Will Change Your Life*.

'In Times of Tragedy' is a blackout erasure poem sourced from Martin Flavin's *Journey in the Dark* (1944), page 15, written on April 15, 2013, the date of the Boston Marathon bombings. It originally appeared on the *Pulitzer Remix* project website.

'I'm Dog. Who Are You?' uses a quote in the epigraph from the article 'In Cambodia, a Middle-Classless Society', from *The New York Times*.

'Nous Sommes Paris' was originally written using text remixed from a CBC News article following the *Charlie Hebdo* shooting in Paris on January 7, 2015. It appeared in *#NousSommesParis* (2016) edited by Oliver Jones, a Special Edition pamphlet commemorating the Paris victims of November 15, 2015 from Eyewear Publishing.

'Our Blood Spans Continents' appeared in *Low Word*.

ACKNOWLEDGMENTS

The idea behind Blackbirds began nearly seven years ago, around the time of the birth of my daughter, and would not have been possible without the help of many, many individuals.

Firstly I would like to thank my family for all their love and encouragement. I am grateful to my mother, Marisol Santos, and late father, Humberto Santos, for instilling in me a love for the arts and reading at a young age. This book is also indebted to my grandparents, who are dearly missed.

Thank you to my mentors, peers, and friends for reading, supporting, and inspiring many of these poems over the years: Gillian Sze, Tammy Ho Lai-Ming, Moe Clark, Stuart Ross, Dean Young, David Lehman, Paul Violi, Honor Moore, and Mark Strand.

Many thanks to my editors Joshua Judson and Todd Swift at Eyewear Publishing for your enthusiasm and belief in this book.

Thank you to my Three Amigos comrades: Joshua Levy, brother writer, for following this shared dream of ours and living it. Thank you to Ryan Schachter for your support and our steadfast friendship.

Thank you to Maryn, my beloved, for being the first reader and editor for much of my writing, and for putting up with years of me following you around with a book in hand as I read to you. Thank you to my dear children, Rosemary and Arthur for always ensuring I stay young at heart. I love you.